By the Lough's North Shore

Paintings by John J. Marshall
Text by Robert Armstrong

Cottage
Publications

First published by Cottage Publications,
an imprint of Laurel Cottage Ltd.
Donaghadee, N. Ireland 2002.
Copyrights Reserved.
© Illustrations by John J Marshall 2002.
© Text by Robert Armstrong 2002.
All rights reserved.
No part of this book may be reproduced or stored
on any media without the express written
permission of the publishers.
Design & origination in Northern Ireland.
Printed & bound in Singapore.

ISBN 1 900935 28 7

Robert Armstrong

Robert Armstrong is a graduate in Local History from St. Patrick's College, Maynooth and the Rural College, Draperstown.

His 30 years work compiling a definitive history of Newtownabbey, *'Through the ages to Newtownabbey'*, 1979, is a credit to him as previously little on the area had been compiled or published. Anyone who has attended his local history courses or joined his historical bus trips will be in no doubt as to his extensive knowledge and enthusiasm. As well as an historian, Bob is also known as an artist, craftsman, sportsman and also as a magician representing Ireland at many International Conventions with his wife as, 'Mentor & Pat'.

Bob lives with his wife Pat and two daughters Nicola and Gail in Newtownabbey and is Secretary of the White House Preservation Trust and the Abbey Historical Society.

John J. Marshall

John Marshall was born in London in 1940. He visited Northern Ireland some 40 years ago and became captivated with the Irish countryside, so much so that he settled here. Apart from being an accomplished artist John is also a talented musician, which resulted in him travelling the world, playing the French horn.

From childhood John was an avid pencil artist. This developed some thirty years ago into oils and subsequently into watercolours. Since, John has gone on to win the prestigious 'European Art Commission Award' for painting and has appeared on the BBC and also Channel 4's programme 'Watercolour Challenge'.

His paintings have been exhibited in Belfast, Dublin and London. Today his paintings increasingly adorn collector's homes not just within Ireland but also as far afield as the USA and Australia.

Contents

Introduction

The Emerald Isle, The Land of Saints and Scholars and the Oul Sod, are only three of the descriptions by which the island of Ireland is acclaimed, each in its own way for good reason. It is approximately 350 miles long by 150 miles wide and recognised as a land of mystery and mythology because until the latter part of the 14th century it was looked upon as the very edge of the world when the earth was believed to have been flat. On its western coast stands the 700ft high cliffs of Mohar that look out on a vast wilderness of ocean with at that time no records or reason for people to believe that any type of land or civilisation lay beyond the horizon. Little did they know that over 11,000 miles distant lay another continent, another world, which would eventually be discovered and named America to become the most powerful and prosperous country on Earth.

Therefore, it is understandable why Ireland is rich in legends and enchantment, where fairies, banshees and leprechauns still roam freely and are ingeniously entwined with a Christian and Celtic culture to produce stories and legends still believed and celebrated to this day.

This book is a celebration of just one small corner of this Emerald Isle. An area which though small in geographical terms, is rich in culture and history as it was the setting of many important episodes in Irish, European and thus world history. This very important strip of land lies along the North Shore of Belfast Lough (Formerly known as 'The Baie of Cragfergus') between Belfast, the capital city of Northern Ireland, in the shadow of the beautiful range of Antrim Hills, via the coast through Carrickfergus, the ancient garrison town

Introduction

of Ulster, complete with its Norman Castle, to the picturesque town of Whitehead. It boasts of an abundance of buildings and features worthy of mention in any publication of this kind. Therefore, it was with great difficulty that these particular examples were chosen. I believe that for various reasons they each hold unique features or fascinations to make them 'special' in the eyes of the artist and historian. It was not sufficient that they had architectural or archaeological significance, but must be pleasing to the eye and tell a story or anecdote of a quality which in some small way may help to interpret the history of the individual people and community who have lived along this shore and inland to include the Six Mile Valley since time immemorial.

The scenes are placed in a geographical manner to enable readers to 'do a tour' starting and ending where they wish, with only a short distance between each site. It is also hoped that each page will act as an incentive to encourage readers to learn more about this beautiful and historical strip of land which is only a small part of this island of beauty.

By means of these beautiful paintings and thoroughly researched historical gleanings each page tells a story, from cabins to castles, from mills to mansions, from wells to souterains, from famous soldiers and sailors to rebels and reparees, from ancient churches to modern tabernacles, from pre-historic burial chambers to battlefields, from musicians to politicians, from poets to mottes and lots, lots more. It was the 'playground' of kings and queens, of patriots and peasants, of warriors and witches.

Whether you travel by foot or car, or even from the comfort of your armchair by simply gleaning through these pages at your leisure why not join us on our picturesque 'Journey through time.'

The People of the North Shore Part 1

It all began around 12,000 years ago when the Ice-Age receded to unveil what we now know as Belfast Lough and the beautiful range of Antrim Hills complete with rugged cliff-faces and the remains of an extinct volcano on the summit of Carnmoney Hill.

5,000 years later, around 7000 BC, nomadic people made their way across Europe searching for a new homeland. There may have been a few land bridges still joining small islands to what we now know as Europe. It is generally believed that man first set foot in Ireland along its Northern coast, probably around Larne, having ventured across the perilous seas in their dugout canoes. They were attracted by the limestone cliffs at White Park Bay and Glenarm. Limestone meant flint for artefacts and weapons, which in turn meant survival.

The island was covered by dense forests of oak, ash and elm with a few coniferous trees so these pioneers probably confined themselves to the coast rather than venture inland where they may have been attacked by wild boar, wolves and other animals. This theory is substantiated by the deposits of the bones of fish and small animals and shells of shellfish found in deposits around our coast.

Although no one will ever know how many of the pioneers lost their lives in that treacherous stretch of water, we can imagine that their only means of transport was sitting astride tree trunks with a determination to reach their goal. Eventually the tree trunks were hollowed, by flint axe-heads worked laboriously from the cliff face, and perhaps a type of sail made from animal skins.

The People

Rivers held a fascination and we know they ventured inland along the Upper Bann, therefore it can only be assumed that their inquisitiveness lead them to explore the little rivers of the Three Mile Water, Six Mile Water and Glas-na-Braden which all flowed into Belfast Lough.

Examples of pottery and flint artefacts are being continuously discovered to remind us of this early period in our country's history. One of the most famous finds is the Ballyclare Hoard which consisted of 39 flint arrowheads in various stages of manufacture, from virtual blank well-worked flints to beautifully constructed arrowheads with 'tangs'.

They were discovered in November 1968 by William E Geary, foreman on a building site at Ballycor Road, who notified the Ulster Museum. Professor Laurence N W Flanagan published a full report in the Ulster Journal of Archaeology, Vol.33, 1970. They are now held by the Museum and put on display periodically.

Arrows made of flint-heads tied by strong plants or animal sinews to small wooden sticks and spears made likewise, were the main means of hunting and fishing. The larger animals were caught in traps or pits, made by digging a deep hole and covering it delicately with a type of trellis using leaves and earth to camouflage it. The animal would then be tempted to accept bait or attack these early settlers thus falling into the pit where they were pummelled to death with large stones.

More visible evidence left by these people for us to admire are their wedge-shaped Court-cairns (one of the finest examples in south east Antrim is described in the section 'Carngraney') and Crannogs.

Crannogs were a type of artificial island deriving its name from 'crann', the Irish word for tree. They were usually constructed in a lake using a base of stones. Onto this base logs and brushwood were piled and as a platform emerged above the water, a stout outer fence of small logs was built on it. One of the finest examples of these defensive constructions can be found in the grounds of Belfast Zoo.

Other reminders of the period include the remains of several souterrains still scattered about the countryside such as those which can be found on Carnmoney Hill, Straid and Doagh. These

Souterrains were originally types of underground dwellings and hideaways come storage facilities to preserve meat. They were made of large flat stones positioned to make a passageway (which varied in length and height) with large cap-stones making a type of stone vault. It would then be covered by earth or dense shrubbery to make it watertight and camouflage it from invaders. Some examples had smaller chambers situated off the main section and the entrance to these souterrains was usually a simple hole in the surface of the ground. If anyone wished to enter they stepped into the hole then usually had to squat or perhaps bow their heads go down another step to enter the passageway or chamber. This left any stranger to the construction at a big disadvantage and open to attack from below as soon as their legs entered the opening. However, unwanted visitors also had means of attack by lighting fires or other materials and tossing it into the chamber to smoke out their 'prey'. One particularly well-preserved example has recently been discovered close by the site of the aforementioned Ballyclare Hoard, proving that this was a densely pupulated area at that time.

Eventually, over a long experimental period, conditions improved considerably with the introduction of domesticated animals and agriculture. However despite these improvements by the 5th century BC these early inhabitants of Ireland were to face stern competition from the invasion of a people whose technology and culture made them well-nigh invincible at the time – the Celts.

These Celts arrived from Europe bringing with them a culture of art and literature that was universally admired. Their jewellery, of which the Tara Broach is a prime example, was in a different dimension compared to anything formerly known in Ireland. Their Fili (storytellers) were the probable ancestors and progenitors in the art of literature for which Ireland, with its many more recent literary geniuses such as Jonathan Swift, Oscar Wilde, Edmond Burke, St John Ervine, Sir Samuel Ferguson, Oliver Goldsmith, Alexander Irvine, Francis Leveridge, James Joyce, Lord McAuley, Thomas Moore, W B Yeats, Seamus Heaney and not forgetting the very talented but much misunderstood Brendan Behan, is now renowned.

It was the Celts who introduced Ogham, the first form of written records known to these islands. It

The People

consists of a series of short straight lines, varying in number and lying at various angles to represent each individual letter. It is read from the base upwards in a vertical line, and it is to be found carved on upright stone tablets throughout the country. A fine example is to be found at Aughascribba, near Greencastle, Co. Tyrone.

The Ogham alphabet revolved round the five fingers of one hand, with each joint and tip being used by the index finger of the other hand a type of pointer, not unlike Deaf and Dumb finger alphabet we know today. There were four letters on each finger, thus totalling twenty letters in all, with five combinations of vowels to represent five foreign sounds. Originally it was a type of secret method of correspondence amongst the Druids, and only began to be used in public, on stones and such, at the decline of Druidism.

These Druids (or Draouthi) were religious leaders and amongst their responsibilities was supervising the coronation of royalty and interpreting the pagan rites towards the worship of numerous Gods and Goddesses one of whom was Brigid, the Goddess of poetry. Given the close proximity of St. Brigid's Well to the great Celtic rath of Dunanney on Carnmoney Hill, who can ignore the possibility that this and many other Christian sites had earlier Celtic connection?

The Celts wore their hair long and used various types of soaps, dyes and cosmetics very generously. Moustaches were a popular trend and in their dress they were fond of bright colours, usually woven in striped or check materials. Both sexes wore a Leine, a tunic of beautifully embroidered linen, worn to the knees by men and to the ankles by women. It was tied around the waist by a criss or belt and over this they wore a cloak of wool held in position by an ornamental broach. Shoes and sandals made from linen with leather soles provided foot protection and some of the lower classes wore a type of trousers.

According to Brehen Law a slave was permitted to wear clothes of only one colour, saffron. A soldier was allowed two colours; a young Lord three; a farmer four; a chieftain five; a poet six and a Queen seven. These regulations resulted in beautifully embroidered robes still to be seen in the costumes used by Irish dancers.

Ornaments of gold, silver and bronze, usually in the form of finger rings, bracelets, ankle rings and belts were of a most artistic and beautiful design, but the most distinctive and beautiful of all their personal ornamentation was definitely the torc, a type of neck collar. These were usually decorated with engraved and embossed patterns and one of the most beautiful, dating from the 1st century AD was found at Broighter, Co. Londonderry.

Women were responsible for rearing the children, the exception being a boy of noble birth, who was reared by a trusted elderly man of the clan, who supervised his warrior and scholastic learning. In later life this admirable custom was reimbursed by the youth who tended to the welfare of his foster-father as a token of respect. These foster-parents were known as Aite and Muime from which some scholars believe we get the words Daddy and Mummy.

Whatever the Celts' undoubted contribution to our culture, today, the most tangible evidence of their civilisation is to be found in the remains of their dwelling places. Their homes were made of stone with a type of thatched roof, and usually built in a prominent position with a good view to spot approaching enemies. They lived as a community within a circular earthen encampment varying in diameter from 30 to 100 metres and usually surrounded by a palisade fence or a deep trench, sometimes filled with water, to help protect them from invaders. These structures are known as raths or forts (sometimes ringforts) and there were once many within this area although unfortunately building developments have destroyed the vast majority. There is one at the rear of Castle High School in Fortwilliam Park, Belfast, known as Fort William (from which the park derives its name) which has associations with a Norman Knight, William de Burgh who was the Earl of Ulster and historically remembered as 'The Brown Earl'. There are also other fine examples of raths at Lisnalinchy, Ballyearl and three quite distinctive ones on Carnmoney Hill. The two smaller are named Ardeen and Knocknenagh, however the most majestic and important in our area is the one known as Dunanney.

Dunanney means 'The Place of the Assemblies' and it got its name because it was originally used as a type of fortress and market-place for the local community. It is of no coincidence that in later years, because of its vantage point, it was used by

The People

Queen Elizabeth's newly appointed Lord Deputy, William Fitzwalter, Earl of Sussex, as a camp for his army of 20,000 troops. At Dunanney he negotiated with several Irish Chieftans, including many who had travelled from throughout Ireland, therefore actually ruling the whole of Ireland from Carnmoney Hill for a full week commencing on 4th August 1556. Dunanney was again used 43 years later (1599) by Robert Devereaux who also encamped here with his army for the same purpose.

But back to the Celts! I think their influence in Ireland is best summarised by O'Driscoll in his History of Ireland.

"Although the Celts didn't found any empires, while other nations converted movable into unmovable property, handed it down in perpetuity and successively added to it by inheritance, the Celtic families went on dividing and subdividing, thus weakening themselves in a weakness chiefly owing to the law of equality and equitable division. As this law of precarious equality has been the ruin of their races, let it be their glory and secure to them at least the pity and respect of the nations to whom they so early showed so fine an ideal".

Despite their dominance in Ireland, the Celts themselves were not immune to cultural change. In the early part of the 4th century, sailors and explorers began to bring back stories of a new religion called Christianity to these pagan shores. The first official mission to Ireland was made by a Christian messenger named Palladious. However his mission was unsuccessful and he died when his ship was wrecked while returning to Rome to give account.

Approximately 30 years before Palladious' mission, Patrick Magonious Sucatus, a youth aged 16 and son of Calpurnius a deacon decurio (an officer in the Roman army commanding ten soldiers) had been snatched from his homeland by Niall of the Nine Hostages the 'Ard Ri' or High King of Ireland. Patrick was made to tend sheep and pigs on Slemish Mountain. After seven years, he either escaped or was given his freedom. It was an acknowledged law that any slave who gave good service to his master for seven years was entitled to his freedom at a nominal fee. He returned to his homeland and tells us in his Confession that he was visited by an angel called Victoricus and told to return to the Irish who needed his guidance in the new-found religion of Christianity. He did so, and is said to have landed in the Wicklow estuary before venturing northwards around the coast to Saul, Co. Down, where he founded his first church in 433AD. Tradition also tells us that in his wanderings he established churches at Shankill (the old church), Skegoniell, Coole, Woodburn, Rashee, Glynne and Magheramorne before heading further south where he lit his pastoral fire on the Hill of Slane and eventually converted Laoghaire the pagan Ard Ri or High King of Ireland. Since then the flame of Christianity has burned brightly in Ireland and because of its internationally known monasteries it became known as the Land of Saints and Scholars. Many monks left these shores to establish religious schools and churches in many European countries and it is said that at one time anyone in the world who could read, write or speak Latin was either taught in Ireland or by a monk who was educated there.

It is recorded that around this time (1000 years before the famous explorers Christopher Columbus or Amerigo Vespucci) an early Irish Christian monk named Saint Brendan ventured across this vast wilderness of sea, defeating unknown and unimaginable dangers to become the first European to land in what we now know as America. The

stories of his voyages are told in the book, '*Navigatio Sancti Brendani*' that became very popular throughout medieval Europe.

Around the end of the 8th century the success of these monasteries, with their wealth of jewellery, including croziers, chalices and beautiful ornate books like the famous Book of Kells, attracted the attention of a race of ferocious sea-faring marauders from the mountainous regions of Scandinavia. They were commonly known as Vikings, which is believed to have been derived from 'Vik' the original Norse word for 'inlet' or 'bay', but were also called Northmen, Norsemen or Danes. They roamed the seas in their longboats and as they began to plunder the Irish coast they found these monasteries to be easy prey.

While there are few, if any, official records of major raids or incursions by the Vikings on the North Shore area, there can be no doubt, given the records of their activities in Bangor and Larne, that they would have explored the various rivers which flowed into the Lough along this shore. In particular the Glas na Bradan (the stream of the salmon) which although only a trickle today because it was diverted to serve the mills, was a substantial river in those days.

Overpopulation and political unrest, combined with a fearless adventurous spirit, saw these pillagers sailing to establish settlements on unknown lands across the vast Atlantic Ocean. At first these missions were unscrupulous raids, striking swiftly and secretly, leaving their unsuspecting victims slaughtered with their homes and lands plundered and in complete ruin. It is said that in the heat of battle they were completely merciless and appeared to go insane; women and children, animals and crops just being wiped out, hence the term 'Berserk' which was the name of one of their most noted warriors.

Their ships were masterpieces of workmanship, being made of wood, which was found in abundance in their homeland. They were deck-less boats, usually measuring a little over 60ft long and were capable of being driven by either sail or oars. Each ship had a fierce looking carved head high on its bow and had a type of rudder at the rear designed to steer it through the narrow fjords of Norway. The combination of sail, oars (which were propelled by a crew of approximately 40 to 60

men) and rudder, with the added advantage of its slim structure, meant it could navigate either vast oceans or shallow streams.

This combination of highly mobile fleets and fierce warriors allowed the Vikings to establish themselves in settlements in various parts of Europe. Often within a few generations, through marriage etc, the descendants of the raiders who set up these settlements became more integrated and settled, along the way developing distinct identities of a more political nature. This was the origin of a new political/military force in Europe who were to have a huge impact on the north shore of the lough – the Normans.

Nestled on the slopes of Cave Hill, 400 ft above sea level, lies Belfast Castle. Offering splendid views of Belfast City and Lough, it stands within the confines of Cave Hill Country Park and was built in the Scottish Baronial style by the 3rd Marquis of Donegall in 1870.

An attractive exterior 'Serpentine Staircase' in classical Italian style was added in 1894 as a present from the 9th Earl of Shaftesbury to his mother. He later became Lord Mayor of Belfast in 1907.

This staircase has proved to be a very popular feature for wedding photographs, likewise the beautiful landscaped gardens based on two themes known as 'The Castle Cat' and 'Nine Lives of a Cat' in remembrance of an actual cat who befriended the gardeners for many years. There are nine references to cats in the immediate vicinity within paving, sculpture and garden furniture which have made a very attractive 'treasure hunt' for visitors both young and old.

Belfast Castle was presented to the City of Belfast in 1934 since when it has been operated as a public building by Belfast City Council Parks & Amenities Department (though not always open to the public such as during WWII when it was occupied by The Royal Navy, particularly the W.R.N.S).

The castle was the subject of a restoration and refurbishment programme which began in 1978 at a cost of £2m over a ten-year period before re-opening on 11th November 1988. The final part of the restoration was completed with the Cellar Restaurant, Bar and Antique Shop, all with a Victorian Belfast shops' design situated in the basement. On the second floor is located the Cave Hill Heritage Centre complete with a remote-control viewing camera where three rooms depict the history of the Castle and its environs. It is therefore an ideal choice for those who wish to go for a casual walk in beautiful surroundings to appreciate the fauna and wildlife, visit the fascinating Heritage Centre or hire this beautiful Castle as a venue for Wedding Receptions, Conferences or Private Parties.

Belfast Castle

Although it is now only a shadow of its former glory and, even at the height of its popularity, may not have had the architectural attributes to compete with many other more illustrious buildings in Belfast, the Floral Hall still holds a very special place in the memories of today's older generation. It was the venue for entertainment of the highest quality including dances, where many young men and women found romance and on numerous occasions their future spouse.

It was originally opened on Monday, 4th May 1936 by the Lord Mayor of Belfast, Sir Crawford McCullagh who in answer to the many critics who doubted its economic viability expressed the view that ….."*a great City like Belfast should not count everything in pounds, shillings and pence nor let the possible absence of profit stand in the way of progress*". He stressed, "*This hall which is on a commanding site, is the answer to a long-felt desire to complete the city's playground to provide an entertainment hall similar in beauty and usefulness to those pleasure resorts across the channel*". It was designed under a constrained budget of £10,000 by Messrs J & R W Taggart, Hopefield Crescent, Belfast at a cost of £9,520 with a further £5,000, agreed with the contractors, towards furnishings and equipment of the very highest standard.

The first show, and forerunner to over 37 years of unparalleled entertainment, was a Variety Concert displaying the cream of local talent. A resident orchestra under the director of Alex Monaghan played regularly.

Thespians were well catered for and Summer Variety shows were much in demand. Likewise, the outdoor festivities of brass bands, Monaghan's orchestra, firework displays by Messrs Brock from Crystal Palace and the very popular dance and community singing which followed, were very well supported, probably because late transport was provided to all parts of the city.

As the popularity of the cinema increased and that of the nearby Zoo, with its many amusement attractions, declined, the Floral Hall gradually lost its popularity and those who attended a dance to Terry Palmer and the Rumble Band on the 4th January 1977 did not realise that they were witnessing the end of an era. The Floral Hall never re-opened as a going concern.

One can only hope that once again in the not too distant future, the strains of music and laughter will be heard echoing around the Cave Hill and across the Ballygolan Lake renowned for its 'Electric duck'. However, that's another story, for another day, known exclusively by the former patrons of the Floral Hall!

The Floral Hall

Loughview Farm is the only place I know, certainly in Co. Antrim, that can boast a famine pot, a George VI post box, an old multi-framed red telephone box, a body-snatchers lamp, ballaun stones, ploughs, scythes and virtually hundreds of farming implements of yesteryear.

It is sited in the Townland of Ballywonard (meaning Town of the High Bog) near the T-junction of Hightown Road and Hydepark Road close to a large modern housing complex, yet as a private dwelling still maintains its exclusiveness that makes it so unique. Cave Hill, Lyle Hill, Big Collin, Little Collin and Carnmoney Hill act as a backdrop to its majestic view of Belfast Lough, hence its name. Even in darkness you are reminded of its location by the intermittent light from the lighthouse on Copeland Islands that lights up one of the bedrooms.

It was originally a long, low thatched cottage built by John Russell in 1820 on 25 acres of land rented from Lord Shaftsbury at £8 per annum, with a clause in the lease claiming an additional 1/- per acre if ploughed.

In 1870 it was modified to a two-storey house to accommodate the Russell family consisting of four sons and two daughters. Shortly afterwards, two of the sons emigrated to Australia and were virtually never heard of again until 1997 when one of the great grandchildren visited his ancestral home.

It was acquired in 1959 by Jack Bristow, who ably assisted by his charming wife Liz pursued the strenuous life of dairy farmers until a few years ago when semi-retirement allowed them to develop their collection of farming implements for personal satisfaction. However, such has been the success of this pursuit that it has grown to become one of the most prestigious private collections in Ireland which school children, tourists and others greatly enjoy.

In recent years the house has only been modified by the addition of a front porch and a conservatory, but old has been cleverly blended with the new during improvements to existing barns and out-houses. It must be emphasised that this is a private farm and may only be viewed by prior appointment. Any visitors who are fortunate enough to be admitted must beware of the 'attention' of the Spinone dogs Harvey and Kane.

Loughview Farm

Midway up the Whitewell Road stands The Throne. A building of great architectural merit when it was designed by Sir Charles Lanyon, it has been changed dramatically by the commercial style shops within its immediate vicinity. It was built and lived in by Sir Samuel Ferguson whom many believe should be accredited with the title of Ireland's national poet. It gets its name because it stood beneath the Throne (the large stone chair) situated on McArts Fort on which Irish Chieftains were crowned for many generations. The remains of this stone may be seen in the Ulster Museum.

Sir Samuel Ferguson was born on the 10th March 1810 at his grandfather's house at 21 High Street, Belfast, educated at the Academical Institution, the leading public school in the city, before proceeding to Trinity College, Dublin, where he graduated BA in 1826, MA in 1832 before being created LLD honoris causa in 1864. In 1838 he was called to the Irish Bar, and obtained practice in the North East Circuit of Ireland before retiring from practice to take up an appointment as Deputy Keeper of the Public Records of Ireland. As the first holder of this office it entailed much investigation and arrangement of documents which were made all the more difficult because Irish Statutes pertaining to the reign of Queen Anne were in Norman/French, a language never used in Ireland since 1495. He thoroughly organised the department into an extremely efficient service and was knighted for his achievements on the 17th March 1878. Sir Samuel Ferguson wrote many well-known poems and literary works, including a book of collected poems entitled 'Lays of the Western Gael' published in 1865.

His most famous work of antiquity knowledge is his 'Ogham Inscriptions in Ireland, Wales and Scotland', which is recognised as a leading work in this field and must have taken long and laborious study to prepare.

He died at Strand Lodge, Howth, in Co. Dublin on the 9th August 1886 from where he was conveyed to the family burial ground in Donegore, Co. Antrim.

The Throne

Not only is this magnificent building of great architectural significance as the largest new church to be built in the British Isles since WWII, it is doubly impressive that at a time when churches of various denominations are finding it very difficult to survive due to dwindling congregations, this particular church has expanded so rapidly that in order to accommodate its followers the building of this 'architectural masterpiece' was an absolute necessity.

No one can deny that such an achievement is because of the dominant, yet charismatic, personality of its founder, Pastor James McConnell who has devoted his life to this church and its congregation, overcoming unbelievable personal and family tragedies and bereavements. One has only got to listen to one of his captivating, yet often controversial sermons to appreciate his gift of 'public communication'.

Several detailed volumes have been written on the life of this great man, in particular '*Light on a Hill*' and '*The Seer's House*', therefore it is suffice to say that from humble beginnings, through being orphaned at an early age and the death of his only sister leaving him virtually alone in the world, James sought and found solace as a 'born again' Christian at the Iron Hall in Templemore Avenue, Belfast, where his grandfather was a regular attendee.

From there he progressed to a little Gospel Hall on My Lady's Road where he gained a reputation as a very talented preacher. After a short spell in England, he returned to use the Orange Hall on the Whitewell Road for a brief period, where he continued to gain local support. Although deeply appreciative for the use of these premises he avoided any 'misunderstanding by association' during the political unrest by building a little church nearby to accommodate his congregation of only ten people.

As this congregation expanded so did his ambitions and yet another much larger church was built on the Whitewell Road. However, because of its success, once again the inevitable happened and after careful discussion between his parishioners and architects, it was decided to build a 'state of the art' Tabernacle based on designs seen on their exploratory trips to America. It cost approximately £5m, paid for by the congregation, and although professionals were needed for the erection of the steel work and other skilled trades, the enthusiastic congregation were continuously on hand to provide the labour. It has been a miraculous achievement and a real credit to Pastor James McConnell and all who attend this Tabernacle.

Whitewell Metropolitan Tabernacle

In the early part of the 19th century the spiritual need of the Roman Catholic community of Greencastle and Whitehouse was nourished by a Priest who travelled by pony and trap once a month from St. Patrick's Church in Donegall Street, Belfast, to administer the Sacraments.

It was found to be inadequate for an area that was growing steadily because of the success of the local mills and their dedicated workforces. Eventually a responsible body was formed to acquire a suitable site for their own place of worship. A kind benefactor named Andrew Nash from Spike Island, Co. Cork (a Catholic) who had married a Protestant named Miss Orr, the daughter of a wealthy landowner, and had settled in one of two large houses known as Seaview Cottages situated on the site of the present Parochial House, presented a portion of his estate to the interested parties for their intended purpose.

The Rt. Reverend Crolly, Bishop of Down and Connor opened the church that is officially known as St. Mary's, Greencastle, on the 20th May 1832. It proved so popular for christenings and weddings that many parishioners even yearned to be buried within its precincts to such an extent that (like the other little local cemetery, Our Lady's Acre) close examination of the head-stones will reveal surnames still familiar in the area even today.

With the growth of the local population, larger premises were acquired and with the purchase and renovation of the nearby Lido cinema, this little church closed in March 1977.

Once again progress prevailed and these premises were replaced by today's modern church on 24th June 2000. Yet the old 'Mother' church still stands albeit unused but most definitely not forgotten because of the important role it played to the many generations of mill-workers, and in its own dignified way still watches over many of them as they 'rest in peace'.

St. Mary's, Greencastle (1832-1977)

The earliest written evidence of The White House is contained in *'a noate'* written in 1574 stating that Queen Elizabeth I gave it to one of her 'gentlemen adventurers' Mr Brunker, because he fought for her in the Spanish Wars. However, it appears to be shown on a map of the *'Baie of Cragfergus'* (the original name for Belfast Lough) in 1569 making it one of (if not the earliest) Bawns in Ireland. It is the oldest surviving building in Newtownabbey, older than any in Belfast by around a century and a half, and derives its name from its white limestone rendered exterior which not only bonded its huge stones but acted as a navigational point of safety for ships entering the treacherous mud-flats and currents of the Lough long before Belfast became a city.

Josiah Martin came to Ireland in the reign of Elizabeth I as one of Chichester's military officers from whom he received many favours. His son (also Josiah) was elected Free Burgess of Belfast and settled at the White House where in 1649 his son George Martin was elected as the first Presbyterian to the honour of Sovereign of Belfast. It is said that he was a loyalist who was intending to join King Charles' army in England and on hearing this information, Oliver Cromwell's party requested permission to billet at the White House. Being refused, the republican troops pillaged the house, seized the goods of Martin and his estates in the neighbourhood and he and his family, which consisted of eight sons, were lucky to escape with their lives, to exile in Scotland.

In later years the infamous Captain Thomas Blood is believed to have used it as a 'safe house' as a guest of Thomas Boyde the owner, and one of his confederates in a campaign of defiance against the English monarchy resulting in the stealing of the Crown Jewels.

On the 14th June 1690 the nearby quay at The White House saw the arrival of 700 ships carrying 35,000 troops belonging to King William III in preparation for the Williamite Wars in Ireland. It is recorded by the King's scribe Gideon Bonevert (after which the nearby park is named Gideon's Green) that His Majesty disembarked at Carrickfergus which was the garrison and principle town in the area before making his way along the hard strand (the beach) to meet General Schomberg at around four o'clock in the afternoon. Unfortunately Schomberg was to be killed a fortnight later at the Battle of the Boyne.

From 1923 to 1967 it was used as a Gospel Hall before being purchased by Ulster Garden Villages on behalf of Abbey Historical Society who through the formation of The White House Preservation Trust, a registered charity, hope to restore it to its former glory to be used as an Educational and Research Centre for Tourists and the local community.

The White House

The area now known as Hazelbank Park is actually an amalgamation of two former houses which occupied prominent positions overlooking Belfast Lough. One was 'Macedon' – formerly owned by John Alexander who named it Macedon so that he would be known as Alexander of Macedon, the famous Warrior. It eventually became a Dr Barnardo's home and was demolished in the early 80s. when the main Shore Road was being widened. The other house was Hazelbank, the home of Thomas McTear, a merchant in Belfast during the 19th century. In an article in the Ulster Journal of Archaeology entitled *'Reminiscences of the Turn of the Century'* he describes a journey from Belfast during the turn of the 18-19th century giving historical gleanings of great houses along the route and their gentlemen owners.

Hazelbank was the family home of James Mackie the industrialist who began business in an iron foundry in Townsend Street, Belfast, repairing parts for textile machinery used in the local mills. He progressed to designing and making the machinery with many of his ideas patented before moving operations to Springfield Road, Belfast, to establish one of the largest privately owned foundries in Europe. During World War II the company gained contracts from the British government to supply munitions and churned out an unbelievable programme of weapons. In its time it was one of the largest employers in Ireland but unfortunately, in parallel with the collapse of the British textile industry, the business became unviable and, despite the best efforts of management and workers it was soon to close.

In 1958 at the formation of Newtownabbey as Rural District Council, Hazelbank was used as its headquarters and Queen Elizabeth II visited it in 1962 during a tour of Northern Ireland. Unfortunately it was bombed in an IRA terrorist attack in the mid 70s and Council business had to be moved elsewhere.

Plans to develop a new Civic Headquarters in the grounds of Hazelbank/Macedon resulted in a Public Enquiry and Judicial Revue in 1993-5 and although the protestors won their case, Mr Tim Smith, Minister of the Environment, overturned the result. In 1996 Newtownabbey Borough Council bought Mossley Mill as its headquarters thus finalising any intention of building administrative premises within the park. This seemed to be a happy compromise and as part of the millennium plan, NBC, in conjunction with government departments, have re-opened the foreshore with a new walk-way and cycle track which incorporates the Ulster Way and is much appreciated by not only people from the Borough but also the tourists.

Hazelbank

In the early part of the 19th century the stretch of shore between Belfast and Carrickfergus was recognised as 'the in-place to build' if you were a gentleman seeking a location for a house. Except for a few interruptions of mill cottages around Whitehouse and Greencastle, and to a lesser extent, Whiteabbey, a series of mansions enabled their owners to enjoy the benefits of the quiet surroundings and beautiful views of Belfast Lough. Thomas Gallaher, Sir Edward Coey, Sir Charles Lanyon, James Mackie, Mr Robinson of Robinson & Cleaver, Mr Anderson of Anderson & McAuley, to name but a few, were typical of the wealthy residents to move into the area.

At Whiteabbey the McCalmont, Cairns and Bland families, all related by marriage, occupied several big houses including Abbeylands, which was destroyed in an arson attack by the Suffragettes in 1912.

Next door is Woodbank. It is said to date from around 1810 but was either rebuilt or completely modified in 1837 when owned by Rev. Robert Wintringham Bland, Dean of St. Georges Church, Belfast, who in turn passed it as an inheritance to General Bland. Three further generations of Blands followed before it was sold to Mr C H Crookshank for £2,000. It passed through ownership of Norman Pringle Metcalfe in 1934 for £1,000 and eventually in 1940 by way of T R L Sinclair for £1,200. Arthur Treffner was the next owner from whom it was

bought in 1963 by Major J M Pinkerton for £6,600 including the market garden.

Although many of these mansions have disappeared the new owners (1963), John and Rosemary Sherlock, have modified the coach house and lodge as well as adding a studio from which John, a renouned international sculptor works. Its facilities include Four Star self-catering accommodation, a private slipway to the beach, secluded patio and barbecue area, extensive lawns and gardens. The recent opening of a new Coastal Marine Walk and Cycle path by the DOE and Newtownabbey Borough Council, stretches from Whiteabbey to Lisburn has given this mansion a new lease of life.

It is little wonder that it is one of the most popular tourist venues along the coast.

Woodbank

The epitaph on the tomb of the distinguished architect Sir Christopher Wren in St. Paul's Cathedral, London, says, *"If you seek a monument look around"*, meaning of course the Cathedral itself, one of his greatest works. Something similar can be said about Sir Charles Lanyon, one of the most influential architects of his time who designed many of Belfast's best-known buildings. Amongst his works is Queen's University, Crumlin Road Courthouse and Gaol, the Custom House, the Palm House in Botanic Gardens, the New Provident Building Institution at the corner of Wellington Place, the Mater Hospital, the Water Office, Belfast Charitable Institution and Campbell College to name but a few.

He was also responsible for the development of the railway lines from Belfast to Ballymena, Bangor, Carrickfergus, and Larne, and also many of the bridges that today span the river Lagan. It is therefore understandable why the directors of the vast network of commercial properties built by Laganbank Developments, which include the Waterfront Hall and the Odyssey, have commemorated his name in the prestigious 'Lanyon Place'.

Born on the 6th January 1813 at Eastbourne, East Sussex, he received his early education in his home-town before moving with his family to Dublin where he became apprenticed to Jacob Owen of the Irish Board of Works and married his daughter Elizabeth Helen. Lanyon was appointed County Surveyor of Kildare and the following year was transferred, at his own request, to County Antrim where he built a well-deserved reputation as an architect and engineer.

The Abbey, which he designed for Richard Davidson M.P. around 1850 stands in the grounds of Whiteabbey Hospital and derives its name from the ancient Cistercian Abbey, which stood nearby from 1215 to 1925 when its remains were wantonly destroyed and removed. It was built on the site of an old thatched cottage called Demrat originally owned by Samuel Getty M.P.

On the death of Getty it was bought by Lanyon who was living in it when he became Lord Mayor of Belfast in 1862. He was also returned as Conservative M.P. making him the third consecutive M.P. to live on the site. In 1868 he became High Sheriff of County Antrim and Deputy Lieutenant and Magistrate of the County. He died in this beautiful old house, now being used as the hospital Administration block, on the 31st May 1887 and is buried in Knockbreda Cemetery, Belfast.

The Abbey

This church known officially as the 'Church of the Holy Evangelists' is known locally as 'Carnmoney Parish' or 'Coole'. It is built on a site that is believed to have been one of a series built along the shore of Belfast Lough which included Shankill (the old church), another around Skegoniell, Coole, Woodburn, Rashee, Glynn and Magheramourne.

The name Coole has been interpreted as meaning a 'mountain pass', which could apply to the valley in which it is built between Cave Hill and Carnmoney Hill. Another is Cuil meaning 'corner' which is equally acceptable because of the corner, which was formed by the Old Irish Highway and Tory Lane. Either way it describes this old important ecclesiastical site dating back to the dawn of Christianity.

Archaeologists and historians are convinced that, although the site has a majestic view, the decision to build an early church, which was probably an old stone thatched building, was because of the existence of an old dependable well, believed to have had healing properties. This well has survived and is thought to have been named after St Brigid, a contemporary Christian missionary of St. Patrick, who is reputedly buried with St. Columba and our Patron Saint at Down Cathedral.

This quaint old well is situated under a little covering archway at the rear of the church. Above it stands one of the most beautiful Celtic crosses in Ireland, built by General Smythe with the intention of placing it as an attraction in the grounds of its sister church, Saint Patrick's which was being built in Jordanstown. However, on his death parishioners felt it more appropriate that it should mark the grave of this great man. It is of Celtic design, 18ft tall with a Crucifixion scene at the base and depictions of the Four Evangelists and entwining Celtic scrolls. Its inscription is written in three languages, English, Irish and Latin and it is most certainly worth a visit.

When appreciating this work of art it is worth considering that one of the highly skilled stonemasons who carved it, with all its delicate and elaborate designs, was Michael Brady, who was executed at Kilmainham Gaol for his part in the murders of Lord Cavendish and his Under-Secretary Thomas Burke in May 1882 in Phoenix Park, Dublin.

Brigid's Well

When the Lancastrian Nicholas Grimshaw founded the first cotton mill in Ireland powered by water, at Whitehouse in 1784, he probably instigated the beginning of the Industrial Revolution in Ireland. He was so successful that many other subsidiary businesses followed quickly, including Carnmoney Print Works under the guidance of Rev. John Thompson and its proprietors a Mr Graham, and brothers Aaron and Moses Stanton. By 1801 Aaron had gained full control and its official name was Aaron Stanton & Company.

Over the next century it changed back and forth between linen and cotton, probably brought about by constant strike action amongst the workers, as was the case throughout the industry in Ireland and England, but also changed ownership on at least four occasions. On the death of Nicolas Grimshaw in 1805 his sons Edmond and Thomas inherited the business at Whitehouse and expanded by acquiring several mills in the area, including in 1821, that at Carnmoney we now know as Mossley.

When and why the name was changed from Carnmoney to Mossley is open to conjecture but in my researches I can find no evidence whatever to substantiate the theory that it was named after Mossley, a little town in England, supposedly the family home of the Grimshaws. They came from Blackburn, and have had commemorative plaques erected to their memory in that locality. Indeed Nicholas was living in the Isle of Man at the time he was invited to Belfast to inaugurate his little business involving orphans and urchins making cravats and white gloves for the gentry, at the Poor House in Clifton Street.

Second cousins, Henry and John Campbell, eventually acquired it. It appears that Henry provided most of the capital and John was the administrator who continued the business after Henry's death and at his bequest opened Campbell College, Belfast, in his memory in 1894. John also expanded the mill, built the village school in 1868 and before he died in 1901 had taken his two sons, Garrett and Howard into partnership. They continued to improve the conditions of the employees by providing recreation facilities and this policy was continued throughout the two world wars.

Expansion continued into the 70s but downturn followed and the mill was closed in 1995. Newtownabbey Borough Council acquired it in 1996 and is at present using it as a Council Civic Centre (opened by HRH Prince of Wales in June 2000) with the intention of including a Museum in Phase II of its development.

Mossley Mill

In the early part of the 18th century a young couple whose families were fierce political rivals were forced to flee from Scotland. Their names were James McKinney, a young highlander who fought with the Stuarts when defeated the previous year (1715) at the Battle of Sherriffmuir and his future wife Helen, of the Campbell clan, who fought on the side of the opposition, the Hanoverians. She was ostracised by her family as a traitor and rebel, so it was in reality a true love story of the Romeo and Juliet type which saw them leave in such a hurry that all they brought with them was a sword and a cooking pot. They were married on the 5th March 1717 in Carnmoney Presbyterian Meeting House and settled at Burnthill on what is now Carnmoney Road.

Their grandson Andrew (a good Scottish name) built a small two storeyed thatched cottage at Sentry Hill, which was replaced in 1835 by the present dwelling. The house and the area get their name from around 1689 when the Expeditionary Forces of William III used it as a lookout post to observe Jacobite manoeuvres in the Lough.

Eventually it was inherited by William Fee McKinney, a keen antiquarian, amateur archaeologist and book collector. He was also one of Ireland's photographic pioneers leaving behind over 3,000 glass slides depicting all aspects of the rural community, including local families and scenes of yesteryear. He accumulated an extensive book collection and had his own little museum containing artefacts ranging from cabinets of stuffed exotic birds, weapons from the 1798 Rebellion and literally thousands of magazines and pamphlets. He also kept a series of diaries and a personal record of births, marriages and deaths in conjunction with holding the office of secretary of the church of his forefathers, Carnmoney Presbyterian Church, for over fifty years.

In later years on inheriting Sentry Hill, W F McKinney's interests were continued by his grandson, Dr Joe Dundee, my close friend, father figure and mentor who shared his inexhaustible knowledge with me on my regular visits for over thirty years, and who, just before he died in 1997 tried to persuade myself and family to come and live with him.

However, through my introduction, Newtownabbey Borough Council acquired it and intends to open it to the public to display all its artefacts as a Museum. That's what Dr Joe would have wanted and when it opens I look forward to a visit when I will most probably still see him sitting in his armchair, drinking his Guinness, with his dog named 'Get out of my road' lying contently at his feet. I dedicate this page to his fond memory.

Sentry Hill Farm

This little cemetery holds many attractions including the grave of Jemmy Hope, the United Irishman and close companion of Henry Joy McCracken. The headstone erected in his memory by Mary Ann McCracken and R R Madden epitomises his honesty and integrity and also bears a carving of an Irish wolfhound.

Nearby is also the last resting place of Francis Joseph Bigger, the author and historian who lived at 'Ardrigh' near the Shaftesbury Inn on the Antrim Road who devoted his life recording history and to whom Ireland owes so much. He tells us in one of his articles that his family used the gravedigger's lamp, which may still be seen, to watch over family graves until rigor mortis meant the bodies were no use for experimental medical purposes. Unfortunately the granite Celtic cross that adorned his grave was destroyed by a bomb during these present 'Troubles' because, I am reliably informed, its epitaph was written in Irish.

One of the most interesting objects to be found here in the northern corner is a fine example of a 'bullaun' stone. No one really knows what these were for but it is generally accepted that in pre-Christian times they were used as a mortar to grind grain and later adapted into ceremonies and rites of both Celtic and Christian religions. This particular example is always full of water and appreciated by visitors where it lies beneath a beautiful yew tree. Closer examination will usually find it contains coins from hopeful 'would-be mums' and others looking for 'favours' as it is reputed to have mystic powers, particularly healing properties.

Local tradition and indeed ancient records and maps seem to suggest that the site was formerly used in early Christian times for religious purposes. In recent years when building houses nearby they found a fine example of a souterrain in the driveway of the house only separated from the cemetery by a hedge. Its neat and tidy appearance is a credit to its owners, Newtownabbey Borough Council.

Mallusk Cemetery

In the townland Craigarogan, mentioned elsewhere in association with the Liberty Tree and Carngraney, stands the remains of an ancient mound, probably originally a Norman motte. It gives its name to the area known locally as Roughfort and, although today it needs urgent attention because of subsidence, is still fondly remembered as a rallying point for the United Irishmen before The Battle of Antrim.

It was only one of a series of rallying points but holds special significance in Irish history because in the early morning of Saturday, 7th June 1798, Henry Joy McCracken, a young Presbyterian patriot who came from a very influential Belfast family, stood on its summit alongside his brother Willy, Jemmy Hope and others to address his men. Only a week earlier he had succeeded Robert Simms as a leader in the North after his sudden resignation and even in that short period had somewhat revitalised and reorganised a depleted 'army' consisting of local farmers who had spent the previous months making pikes and 'make-do' swords for what was referred to as 'the turn out'.

It was yet another beautiful sunny day in the long hot summer that had provided a good harvest and many wives and mothers escorted their men-folk to the gathering at the 'oul fort'. Initially only around 50 men assembled but the numbers were swelled suddenly by a large contingent from Carnmoney before they formed ranks, musketeers in front, pike men in the centre and the solitary canon mounted on a common car at the rear as they set off toward Antrim to the tune of the ' *The Swinish Multitude*'.

Children who didn't realise the seriousness of the situation joined in behind the ranks, or attempted to join their fathers, but were ushered away by their mothers, many of whom were in a state of despair with tears flowing freely.

The rest is history – victory was snatched from their grasp after they had gained the advantage in a hard fought battle in the town of Antrim. The depleted 'Summer Soldiers' sought refuge in the countryside including Slemish Mountain but eventually Henry Joy McCracken was tried and executed in Belfast on the very ground which his grandfather Henry Joy had presented to the town.

Roughfort

At a time when France, Ireland and America were seeking independence, Thomas Payne wrote in his 'Rights of Man', *"You have nothing to fear but fear itself - throw off your chains"*. It was a period of great activity which eventually saw America gain independence from Britain in 1776, ably assisted by many Ulster-Scots who had helped to pioneer the country and took the opportunity to acquire for their new homeland what they had failed to do in Ireland. The French Revolution followed in 1790 and although Ireland's failed in 1798 it did eventually gain independence around a century later.

Throughout this period of uncertainty symbols became a means of injecting patriotism into the hot-blooded pioneers of the New World. In France it was the guillotine, Ireland the harp and shamrock and in America, the bald eagle, but one thing they did have in common was the need for a means of communication at a time when there were very little newspapers or media, as we would know it today. It was therefore inevitable that the venue would be found to keep people up to date on the news of the happenings in their quest for independence. What better means of communication would be than a tree, a living emblem of beauty and determination, spreading its branches as if in defiance of authority? It was on chosen trees, usually situated in the centre of a village or town, Proclamations were posted and they became known as Liberty trees. In America yellow ribbons were tied on these trees as a token for the safe return of those away from home. The last liberty tree in the USA dating back to the time of the Independence was only cut down in the late 1990s.

Our Liberty tree stands in the townland of Craigarogan, only a matter of yards from the Roughfort where Henry Joy McCracken and his band of patriots gathered before the Battle of Antrim. Said to have been planted in the year of the first anniversary of the Uprising it stands majestically as a beautiful testimony to the memory of the Presbyterians and Catholics who walked side by side in the 1798 Rebellion in Antrim.

The Liberty Tree

What might look like an old 'pile of stones' lined in the middle of the field adjacent to the Liberty Tree, is in fact acknowledged as one of Northern Ireland's most notable archaeological sites. It is known locally as 'Granny's Grave' and officially as Carn Graine or Carngraney, meaning 'a cairn of the sun' and is a wedge-shaped nine or ten chambered cairn dating back over 6000 years. The Ordnance Survey Memoirs of 1838 says, *"Within the memory of some old people, this temple was enclosed by two circles of standing stones, which were from 2-3 feet high; the inner circle was about 35yds and the outer 60yds in diameter, the stones were at some distance from each other. It is almost 50 years since these stones were destroyed but since that period the temple has not undergone any change"*. As this was written in 1838, the date referred to must have been around 1788.

Bishop Reeves in his Ecclesiastical Antiquities (page 66) describes it as being a series of cromlechs commencing in the northeast and ascending gradually for a length of 40ft towards the southwest. The largest stone is raised 7ft or 8ft and is 6ft 9inch x 5ft broad x 2ft thick. The smallest, on the ground is 5ft long by 3ft 3inch broad.

Each of these descriptions are of interest in their own right, but perhaps the most complete study was published in 1914/16 by H C Lawlor who, with the assistance of Rev W P Carmody and Lt. J H Lawlor, numbered the chambers from the front, 1 to 9 for convenience and described each in detail. To summarise, Chambers Nos.1, 4,6,7,8 and 9 were examined either partially or completely. Chambers Nos.2, 3 and 5 would have necessitated the removal of the top stones which in their opinion would have been vandalism. All the chambers entered with the exception of Nos.1 and 9 displayed examples of cremations without urns; No.1 had previously been 'investigated', showed nothing, No.9 gave evidence of two interments, one or both being urn burials into soil after cremation. Although one urn had disappeared the other remained intact (somewhat briefly) and had to be repaired by a Mr W F Cox of India Street.

This beautiful encrusted urn is now in the Ulster Museum. Farmers have removed all the surrounding 'standing stones' over the centuries as they ploughed the field. Some of the 'cap-stones' have caved-in but yet this 'old pile of stones' (registered as a listed monument by the DOE) somehow holds a mysterious fascination for inquisitive visitors.

Carngraney

At the end of WWI a meeting was called on the 29th November 1918 by the High Sheriff of Co. Antrim, Mr Henry Barton, of The Bush, Co. Antrim, to discuss a proposal to erect, on a site to be decided, a monument worthy of the memory of the men from the county who had been killed in action.

He was appointed Secretary of a committee that was formed to oversee the task with instructions to erect an obelisk in local basalt with bronze panels listing the names of the casualties. Knockagh was chosen from a list of suitable hills and ways to raise the cost, estimated to be in the region of £25,000, were examined.

Subscriptions were very slow to arrive and by 1921 only £1,834 had been raised, probably due to many towns and villages deciding to erect their own local memorials.

Barton remained committed and in April 1921 land was purchased from Mrs Jane McAuley of Knockagh for the obelisk, with additional land for an approach road. Over a hundred invited guests attended the laying of a foundation stone by Lady Antrim on the 7th October 1922. The design was based on the Wellington Monument in Phoenix Park, Dublin, a striking 205ft tall obelisk designed by Sir Robert Smirke and completed in 1817. It was intended that the Knockagh Monument would only be half its height at 110ft with bronze panels for inscriptions. Eventually these proved too expensive and were replaced in the design with a simple laurel leaf in bronze placed 10ft above the plinth with 1914 – 1918 shown. Afterwards this was added to with 1939 –1945 in remembrance of the fallen heroes of World War II

By the time Henry Barton died in 1934 he had contributed £6,428 of his personal money towards his dream but the surfacing of the road and installation of iron gates and railings had still to be completed. Antrim County Council took on responsibility for the work to completion and was later assisted financially by the other Borough Councils of the county in 1984 towards the expense of its renovation.

The inscription on this great monument is taken from the hymn O' Valiant Hearts by John S Arkwright–

"Nobly you fought, your knightly virtue proved,
Your memory hallowed in the land you loved".

On reflection this quotation also seems quite appropriate to the memory of Mr Henry Barton who, in the company of Co. Antrim's fallen heroes, will never be forgotten while this great monument stands.

The Knockagh Monument

Visitors travelling by road from Belfast to Carrickfergus will need a keen eye to find the site of Castle Lug which stands near the shore at Greenisland, just within the southern boundary of Carrickfergus Borough Council.

It was originally known as Cloughlougherty, and later Cloughnaherty and is believed to have been built on this site to conveniently oversee and protect Carrickfergus and its castle from any invasions by the Clandeboye O'Neill's from Castlereagh.

In reality it is not a castle but one of a series of Tower-houses (like others at Whitehead, Larne etc) and although it cannot be proved, probably derives its name from the Lugge Family who were very influential in local politics in the 16th-17th centuries as Burgesses, Sherrifs and Mayors of Carrickfergus. In 1574 John Lugge was granted all *'the castles, halls and other herediments of Thomas Lugge',* his grandfather, once Burgess of Carrickfergus.

Recent excavations nearby suggest that like other known examples, it probably had closeby, one or two accompanying Tower-houses joined by an escarpment wall.

Today it is well-tended by Historic Monuments and Buildings branch of the DENI.

Castle Lug

During the 6th century Fergus, the son of Eric of Armoy, left Ulster to form a kingdom in what is now known as Scotland but because he suffered from leprosy he returned from time to time to bathe in a well which apparently had healing properties. On one of these visits he was shipwrecked on the rock on which the Castle is built thereby creating the name 'Carrickfergus', meaning 'the rock of Fergus'. It is believed that the well is the one still surviving within the Castle.

Five centuries later King Henry II encouraged Anglo/Norman knights, who had vast military experience in the Crusades in the Holy Land, to attack Ireland and confiscate land in his name to increase his kingdom. One of these knights was John de Courcy, renowned for his merciless ferocity on the battlefields of Europe and within a short period had established himself as Earl of Ulster. In an effort to become more acceptable to the Irish he built Abbeys to accommodate their deep religious convictions and Castles to defend his own personal interests. However, he fell out of favour with King Henry II when he appeared to be establishing his own little kingdom by producing his own coinage and was replaced by Hugh de Lacy who is credited with the completion of the Castle.

Over the next 750 years the occupancy of the Castle changed hands several times in a succession of sieges that saw it inexorably linked with important European events. King John seized it from De Lacy in 1210 but De Lacy recaptured it in 1227 as part of his restored title, Earl of Ulster. He died here in 1242. Edward Bruce, brother of Robert the legendary King of Scotland, besieged it for over a year in 1315 and after the collapse of the Earldom of Ulster in 1333, the Castle remained the Crown's principal residential and administrative centre in the north. It was subject to other notable attacks, in 1386 and 1402 when the Scots destroyed much of what was the original walled town, as did Sir Phelim O'Neill of Clandeboye in 1575 and Sorley Boy O'Donnell two years later.

The importance of Carrickfergus Castle in a international context is epitomised by the involvement in its story (at various times) of a German General (Fredreich Schomberg), a former Dutch Prince (King William III), a French Commodore (Thurot) and an American Privateer (John Paul Jones) who is credited with being the 'founding father' of the American navy.

Carrickfergus Castle is generally recognised as being Ireland's finest castle and is today a major tourist attraction. Refurbishment is currently being undertaken to restore its ancient stonework.

Carrickfergus Castle

Of all the subjects included in this publication, without doubt the smallest yet the most controversial is the statue of King William III that stands in the grounds of Carrickfergus Castle.

It was sculpted by Mr Edward Barton who was commissioned by Carrickfergus Borough Council to provide a life-size bronze statue to commemorate the tercentenary of His Majesty's landing at the castle on 14th June 1690 and unveiled accordingly exactly 300 years later in 1990. For almost a year he studied all known aspects of the King's physical features, including his dress and mannerisms. He discovered that William suffered from a curvature of the spine, which meant he had a very short thickset neck, wore a Dutch wig (usually very tight curls, unlike the English and French with long flowing tresses) and was between 5ft 5ins and 5ft 6ins tall.

It was important that the sculptor knew how the figure was to be displayed, on a tall plinth or at ground level, when deciding its height to avoid any perspective illusion and it was agreed that it would be sited on a 3ft plinth with the immediate area landscaped accordingly. However, because of the tight time schedule of the celebrations, the statue was finally displayed about 5ft higher than originally planned. The result is an illusion of height creating the impression that William was a 'dwarf'. This has been the subject of comments and discussions ranging from favourable and admirable comments about the detailed skill with which Edward Barton sculpted the actual figure to cruel jibes about its size.

A story worth relating is told by Mervyn McDowell a Carrick official and local historian about a visit from an Orange lodge to Carrickfergus to see and hear about its tourist attraction. Midway through his talk he was interrupted by one of the visitors who complained about the 'size' of the statue. Mervyn thanked the gentleman for his astute observation saying *"I can only apologise on our behalf because, as we all know, the sculptor created it an inch too tall!"* And believe it or not, it is an inch too tall – and for those who doubt me all I can say is … *"It's an optical illusion".*

William III Statue, Carrickfergus

By the middle of the 13th century the Norman invasion of Ireland was subsiding and being gradually accepted. One of the ways in which this was achieved was by playing on the Christian sympathies of the people of the island by building monasteries, abbeys and other religious institutions.

In 1232 Hugh de Lacy, Governor of Carrickfergus Castle and Earl of Ulster, founded a Franciscan Friary on the site of what is now Carrickfergus Town Hall thus beginning a very interesting history of this particular site. It enjoyed over 300 years of virtual stability (peace) until 1560 when most of the monasteries were destroyed by order of Henry VIII who had formed the Church of England, henceforth to be recognised as the 'new established' church.

In 1599 the lands passed to Sir Arthur Chichester who built Joymount Palace, often described as one of the finest houses in Ireland, on the same location. It was demolished in 1768 but the remains of one of its towers can still be seen in the yard at the rear of the Town Hall.

The same site was utilised eleven years later by the erection of the County of Antrim Courthouse and Gaol, to the design of Richard Drew at a cost of £5,785. 6s. 4d. Between 1815-1856 several additional wings, a chapel, a bath, gaolers lodge, guardroom and execution room were added and alterations made to accommodate the Staff of the Royal Antrim Artillery and Royal Antrim Rifles.

It was at this site in 1711 the last trial in Ireland regarding 'Witchcraft', involving ladies from nearby Islandmagee, took place. Also that of Eneas O'Haughan, the notorious highwayman whose head, just like those of his three brothers, was displayed on a spike on the gaol wall.

However, this Courthouse is best remembered as the venue for the trial of William Orr, which took place in October 1797, before his execution at the Gallows Green.

The building and its immediate environs underwent several alterations and demolitions until Carrickfergus Urban District Council bought it in 1934. Messrs Samuel Stevenson and Messrs William Logan & Sons Ltd, Belfast, were the architects and builders respectively. A new chapter in the history of this site was written on 11th July 1935 with its official opening as Carrickfergus Town Hall, by the Prime Minister of Northern Ireland, Lord Craigavon.

Carrickfergus Town Hall

About a mile north of Carrickfergus lies the little hamlet of Boneybefore, famous as the ancestral home of Andrew Jackson (1767-1845) who served two terms (1829 to 1837) as the 7th President of the United States who was affectionately known as 'Old Hickory' and 'The People's President'.

Although the actual cottage was demolished in the 1860s to make way for the railway, a blue commemorative plaque marks the site. A neighbouring cottage, built by an Ulster Scots family named Donaldson around 1750, was purchased by Carrickfergus Borough Council in the 1970s and has been furbished with furniture and equipment of the period to depict the life and career of President Andrew Jackson, the Ulster Jackson's and Ulster's connection with North America.

It is known as the Andrew Jackson Centre in appreciation of the life of this great man. He was orphaned at the age of fourteen and rose from virtual obscurity, having been born in a log cabin, to be recognised as one of America's greatest sons.

He is remembered as the father of the Democratic Party and after an eventful career as a lawyer, senator, judge and major general in the Tennessee militia he became a national hero by defeating the British at the battle of New Orleans in 1815. He died on the 18th June 1845 at 'The Hermitage', Nashville, Tennessee.

Also included within the confines of this Centre is an exhibition of photographs, uniforms and artefacts donated by, and dedicated to, the US Rangers. The first battalions of this elite force were Volunteers from other US Army units located in Northern Ireland who were based at Sunnylands Camp, Carrickfergus, for their initial training and induction.

Major William O. Darby was appointed as their first commander and on 19th June 1942 the Rangers were officially activated as a combat unit. The Rangers' task was to act as a 'Spearhead' force for the invasions during WWII; a job it still continues with the American forces throughout the world today.

The Andrew Jackson Centre

Situated at Kilroot, within the boundaries of this vast parkland demesne there stands evidence of three buildings, all successively known as Castle Dobbs or Dobbs' Castle. In 1610, *"One John Dobb buylte a fayre castle within two myle of Knockfargus called Dobb's Castle"*. By 1683 Richard Dobbs refers to *"the small castle built by my grandfather"*. This building still stands in ruins adjacent to the 'next' Dobb's Castle of which only foundations remain.

The present house was built around 1750 to 1754 and is described by Professor Rowan, *"It is without equal in Ulster while its perfect Palladian plan with flanking wings – if from a pattern book source – is hard to match in a house of this scale anywhere in Ireland"*. Arthur Dobbs, the original owner of this latest building, was surveyor of Irish Works before emigrating to become Governor of North Carolina.

In 1752 it is recorded by a Mr Pococke, *"Mr Dobbs is now building on a very fine spot of rising ground"*. Almost a hundred years later James Boyle in 1839 said *"the house is a spacious old-fashioned looking mansion, the entrance presenting in its central building and two projecting wings a somewhat Elizabethan appearance. It is three storeys high and presents a plain roughcast and whitened front – plantations, grounds and house are in a very neglected state"*.

Sir Charles Brett describes it in his excellent book *'Houses of County Antrim'* (1995) in his usual meticulous manner as *"Basically, this is a rather large 7-bay 2-storey double-pile house, on a substantial basement, with two 5-bay 2-storey wings without basement, linked by courtyard quadrants lit by pairs of oval lunettes. The south-facing façade, with 33 windows, but no other opening, door, porch or portico, is formidably austere. The simple pediment on the south face, the hipped roof with four solid chimney stacks, consort a bit uncomfortably with the Victorian frills below. Much of the original internal joinery and some fine plasterwork, survive"*.

Even considering all its additions, improvements and architectural irregularities, this house is a most striking residence, enhanced greatly by the beautiful pond and parkland boasting of a range of trees including a series of splendid oaks that were planted before the house was built.

It is still occupied by descendents of John Dobbs, a family that has served Carrickfergus in many capacities with a history as fascinating as their castle – or should I say castles?

Castle Dobbs

Ballynure, meaning 'the town of the Yew trees' known otherwise as Toberdowney, has many places of interest and associations with many famous people including Mark Twain, (Samuel Leghorn Clements), the author of Tom Sawyer and Huckleberry Finn; Sam Houston, first President of the Lone Star state of Texas and Jonathon Swift, famous for the classic Gulliver's' Travels.

Dean Swift was based at Kilroot from 1694 to 1696 with Ballynure as part of his parish served by the small church, the remains of which may still be seen in the centre of what is now the local graveyard. It is recorded that he had great difficulty in acquiring a congregation because most of the locals were Presbyterians. In an attempt to swell the numbers he used the field adjoining the church/graveyard for outdoor services, hence the 'Preacher's Green' name still used today.

However, it is ironic that in 1797 the opposite was the case when the village Presbyterian Meeting House was full to capacity for the service and wake of William Orr, the United Irishman who was hanged at Carrickfergus for his involvement. He was the first 'patriot' to meet this fate and such was the public sympathy and outcry that the battle cries at Antrim, Saintfield and Ballynahinch during the Rising the following year was, 'Remember Orr'.

The churchyard holds the graves of many notable families like Dobbs and Ellis whose names are synonymous with the history of Carrickfergus, and of course that of the Rev. Adam Hill who put his own life at risk by defying the law to administer the service to Orr.

Just inside the gates of the churchyard stands a large stone vault which was used to store bodies in safety from 'body-snatchers' till rigor mortis had set in and they were of no use to this sordid yet very profitable profession.

Close by is a grave surround with a 3ft high wall topped by a 3ft high railing with a sliding centre portion used for the convenience of putting coffins through for burial, yet when locked act as a deterrent to these 'midnight marauders'.

Probably the most intriguing feature in the churchyard is the archway above what was the original main door to the church with its self-supporting keystone displaying the skills and ingenuity of a by-gone age. How long it can remain supportive of the heavy stones is questionable and I hope the responsible bodies take it upon themselves to secure it for the admiration of future generations before it is too late.

Ballynure Churchyard

In the early years of the 18th century an old wooden building was erected in 'the square' at Ballyclare to serve as a Market House for the convenience of linen merchants who otherwise had to travel to Belfast. It served its purpose well but, in the interests of progress and to accommodate this ever-growing profession, it was replaced in 1866 (at a cost of £480) by a stone building. The cost was borne by public subscription.

Around seven years later in 1873 a Town Hall was built on top of the Market House at a cost of £500, again borne by public subscription, with separate committees for each to look after their affairs. Eventually a serious disagreement arose between the parties that resulted in a lawsuit in the King's Bench, Dublin, in 1913, the outcome of which a Trust was formed to take control of all the building.

It is recorded that wooden planks on trestles served as a 'stage' for the use of artistes who soon learnt through several accidents, not to move around too much during their performance.

Dances proved the most popular form of entertainment, usually commencing about 9.30pm and often continuing till 5.00-6.00am the following morning with many of the participants going straight to work at the local mills. The 'orchestra' was usually comprised of a couple of fiddlers, a melodeon, a flute and if lucky, a piano.

Throughout their frolics the patrons of the dances were inundated by the odour of dead pigs, bacon and butter from the shadows of the Market House underneath.

In recent years this grand old building served as the headquarters of Newtownabbey Borough Council, utilising the upper storey as the Council Chamber. Since the Council moved to Mossley Mill an active committee has acquired it once again for the benefit of the people of Ballyclare and district and it is ironic that the first official function to be held was a very, very successful dance – with many more likely to follow.

Ballyclare Town Hall

No one can be sure when this fine man-made structure was built. It may have been the original site of a rath, but more than likely it first saw 'the light of day' around the 12th – 13th centuries when Ireland was invaded by the Normans. The purpose of these structures, which were easily built, was to gain a prominent position from which they could conquer and control areas of the countryside. There were hundreds scattered throughout the island with over 70 recorded in County Antrim. Their sizes varied considerably but they were usually around 5 metres high and 20-25 metres in diameter across the summit, often encircled by a ditch.

Mottes were often built at strategic points to secure lines of communication, especially valley routes, and often had an additional 'bailey', which was an enclosure usually slightly lower and enclosed from where its inhabitants, including cattle and other domesticated animals, could be viewed.

Their popularity declined around the 13th century when any mottes of particular strategic importance were replaced by buildings of stone, even sometimes being replaced by castles.

The Ballyclare Motte was probably positioned to overlook the river still known locally by its original name of The Ollar, later becoming The Six Mile Water because when soldiers were marching along its banks between the garrison town of Carrickfergus and its counterpart at Antrim, when they reached this area they had marched six miles.

This motte has recently seen great changes within its confines as workmen re-routed the river to make way for the facilities of the splendid Six Mile Leisure Centre.

This blend of ancient and modern should be used as an example to planners and environmentalists who too often seek 'progress' at the expense of our heritage.

Ballyclare Motte

Standing in the main street of Doagh, opposite the Ballyclare Road is an obelisk erected to the memory of John Rowan who died on the 19th July 1858. He constructed a steam coach in 1836 and drove it through Belfast where he had set up his agricultural machinery and boiler making business in York Street (on the site which became Gallahers and subsequently Yorkgate Shopping Centre).

To put this feat in its proper perspective of importance it must be remembered that 'Stevenson's Rocket' had only been invented seven years earlier and the only known means of road transport was a horse and cart, therefore it must have been one of the earliest road vehicles, and the forerunner to the motor car. Unfortunately, like Stevenson's Rocket it was not a commercial success, but John Rowan continued to use his inventive brain and skills as a craftsman to invent something that revolutionised transport, the piston ring. He advertised these extensively with great success.

The inscription on this obelisk confirms his generosity and personal relationships with his employees who held him in very high esteem.

Rowan Monument

The little village of Ballycarry, formerly known as Broad Island and made famous in the song sung by Richard Hayward, *'The Mutton Burn Stream'*, written by William Hume, (grandfather of local historian Dr David Hume) boasts proudly that it was the site of the first Presbyterian Church founded in Ireland.

The Rev. Edward Brice, a gentleman who came to Ireland from Scotland as one of the persecuted who practised this religion, instigated the Church in 1613. The remains of the old church still stand with a commemoration plaque marking the grave of its Founder on its eastern interior wall.

Within the confines of this graveyard are many other graves of interest and what makes it so original is that it is laid out with coloured markers, complete with display board to enable visitors to find them easily. One of the most ornate and popular is that of James Orr known locally as the Ballycarry Bard and renowned for his many poems depicting important and everyday episodes in the life of this little village. One of his best known is *'Donegore Hill'* relating to the Battle of Antrim in 1798. Close by is the last 'resting place' of James Burns with a fascinating cryptic epitaph using numbers instead of letters to relate a portion of scripture. An explanation plaque is provided.

Also, nearby is that of young Willie Nelson, a boy of 18 years of age who was hanged by the English militia for his part in riding round the countryside encouraging farmers and local inhabitants to lay down their scythes and farming implements and head for the Battle of Antrim. He was hanged outside his mother's door and left as a warning to other sympathisers within the village.

As he was looked upon as a 'traitor and criminal' the law forbid any type of grave identification or epitaph (although it was well identified in local tradition). It was only recently that historians had the opportunity to commemorate the bi-centenary of this uprising by placing plaques on the graves of these 'patriots' – Henry Joy McCracken at Clifton Street new burial ground, William Orr at Templepatrick and others.

As an historian and fully appreciative that this is a very much misunderstood period in Irish history I take great satisfaction and consolation in the fact that many Councils and organisations regardless of political or religious persuasion commemorated the bi-centenary of the 1798 Rebellion.

It's better late than never.

Ballycarry Churchyard

In March 1898, the Secretary of the Board of Trade, speaking in the House of Commons, confirmed his agreement with the decision of the Commissioners of Irish Lights, that a light and fog signal at Black Head would only be for the benefit of local traffic and was therefore outside the financial liabilities of the Mercantile Marine Fund.

A month later at a meeting of the Belfast Harbour Board, Captain Molyneaux, the Harbour Master, emphasised the need for such a signal by reading out a long list of shipping disasters in the immediate area. He explained that although there was a long stretch of shore without any light or fog signal, the proposed site was eight miles outside the harbour limits and therefore outside their jurisdiction. However, he continued to say that the Belfast Chamber of Commerce had given additional reasons to the Commissioners of Lights by asking them to take into consideration that Belfast Harbour was mainly a harbour of refuge. He stated that the Commission was now prepared to give the application renewed consideration.

Common sense prevailed and it was finally opened on 'April Fool's Day' in 1902 and the first appointed Chief Lighthouse Keeper was Mr E A Kennedy. It stands 51ft high, 148ft above high watermark and was originally painted red.

The lighthouse had only been in operation a short time when several captains complained of another light in the town of Whitehead flashing with the same frequency. An investigation by an official of the Irish Lights discovered that the beam from Black Head lighthouse was being reflected by a large mirror in the bedroom of a house in York Avenue. The occupant of the house vehemently refused to either move the mirror or close the blinds, because he argued that the seaward side of the town should not be constantly subjected to the sweep of the beam. Alterations were subsequently made to the lighthouse to stop it flashing on any part of Whitehead.

Therefore, in reality what we have today is a very familiar landmark which people fought to achieve yet in a way had to be 'hidden' from their view.

Black Head Lighthouse

The People of the North Shore Part II

The people known as the Normans originated from a Viking settlement on the north coast of France which expanded to control large tracts of what is now known as Normandy. Over the next two centuries from this base they became the dominant force in Europe and, under their leader William the Conquerer, conquered England in 1066. A century later William's descendant, Henry II, despite being the unchallenged ruler of both England and large parts of France, was intent on expanding his kingdom. Thus when he was approached by Dermot MacMurrough of Ireland who was seeking assistance after being driven out of his Kingdom in Leinster by Rory O'Connor, the King of Connacht who had just been appointed High King of Ireland, Henry was quick to spot an opportunity.

He quickly gave permission for a number of Norman knights to assist Dermot, the chief among these being Richard Fitzgilbert, better known, due to his military prowess, as Strongbow.

Landing in Ireland in 1170, Strongbow was followed by several other Norman knights who found the Irish clans no match for their military expertise gained on the battlefields of Europe and The Holy Land Crusades. Horse warfare, complete with chain-mail, visors, swords and lances were the means of confiscation of land and property by these warriors

Such was their success (after Dermot died in 1171 Strongbow declared himself King of Leinster) that Henry became concerned that Strongbow was preparing to break away and declare independence. To forestall this, Henry landed in Ireland in October with 4,000 troops. Strongbow, realising that he was overmatched, pledged his allegiance to Henry who, in return, permitted Strongbow to continue ruling Leinster. However, to prevent Strongbow again gaining a too dominant position, Henry in a policy of 'divide and rule' encouraged other Norman knights to come to Ireland in search of land and wealth.

One such knight was John de Courcy. It is said that Henry II mentioned casually to him that, provided he maintained his allegiance to the English Monarchy, he could rule over any of the area of north-east Ireland which he could conquer as 'Earl of Ulster'. This tall, fair-haired young Norman didn't need any persuading. He was quite poor, but had built up an unbelievable reputation on the battlefields of Europe.

"Few men could match DeCourcy on saddle or on sword.
The ponderour mace he valued more than any Spannish sword.
On many a field of slaughter, scores of men lay smashed and stark,
And the victors as they saw them said 'Lo!',
John DeCourcy's mark"

De Courcy landed in Dublin in 1176 and by 1177 had gathered an army of some 300 with which he invaded Ulster. Initially he was in constant conflict with the native tribes but his military prowess soon meant that he held sway over most of the Province. He then set about a process of consolidating his position, part of which was to appease the Irish. He married Affreca, the daughter of the King of the Isle of Man and built several castles and beautiful cathedrals. Some of the finest examples surviving are the castles at Dromore, Dundrum and Carrickfergus and the abbeys and churches at Inch, Greyabbey and St. Nicholas's at Carrickfergus. Further tapping into the Irish love of religion, he minted his own coins which bore the likeness of St. Patrick on one side and his own on the other.

Unfortunately for De Courcy, his success in this venture (as with Strongbow earlier) aroused the suspicions and jealousy of his peers and Monarch. The success with which he kept back the O'Neills and kindred tribes from the principality he had carved out for himself was probably his eventual undoing.

The De Lacys, who had land in Meath and were

covetous of his title accused him of high treason and the Earldom was granted to Hugh de Lacy who was instructed by King John to capture De Courcy.

As I have stated elsewhere De Courcy was no ordinary man, in either physique or military expertise, so to capture him was no easy mission. He received word that an attempt on his life was imminent and retreated to his castle at Dundrum where he defeated De Lacy in battle. Later that year in 1204 De Lacy realised he couldn't defeat such a mighty warrior as De Courcy who had overcome many during his lifetime, so he bribed De Courcy's friends to betray him. How he was captured is worth relating so I quote Hammer.

"His servants were bought over by his enemy and this advice his betrayers gave, 'Sir, John De Courcy is a mighty man in arms and of such strength that no one dares to be so hardy as to lay hands upon him; and again he is always, both in public and provided, yet we can direct you a course to bring your purpose to effect. Upon Good Friday yearly he wears no arms but is wholly given to Devine contemplation and commonly walketh all solitary around about the churchyard of

Down; if you provided a troop of horsemen in readiness and send your espiall before, there you shall have him, apprehend him and work your will'. And hither they came and laid hands upon him. De Courcy, now unarmed and altogether distressed ran to a wooden cross that stood in the churchyard and took a pole thereof and laid about him lustily'.

To be short the author of the Book of Howth reports sarcastically that: *"De Courcy slew 13 that died not on the cross, but under the cross."*

He was taken to the Tower of London but was obviously too valuable a warrior to be disposed of and he was later released to act as champion against a French knight of King Philip's. When the Frenchman saw his huge opponent armed with his trusty sword which had already seen violent action in Ireland, he fled petrified. It is believed that De Courcy died about 1219.

Orpen says that:

"The life of John De Courcy is like a wild romance and would hardly be believed were it not

The People

On reflection I feel that Ulster, and of course the north shore of the lough in particular, owes a great deal to this Norman Earl. He used strength to subdue any possible coups but also established places such as Carrickfergus, Downpatrick, Dundrum and Dromore around which new types of towns evolved. Money was in use for the first time and I personally can't help but think that as a whole, good came out of his reign. It also sets me thinking that another great man was betrayed by his friends, seized when least expecting it in a garden and although our Lord gave no resistance, He was crucified on the same fateful day – Good Friday. Such was the impact of this knight-adventurer on this area that his silver and white armorial colours are represented to this day in the coat of arms of the modern Borough of Newtownabbey.

After De Courcy's betrayal Hugh de Lacy was named as his successor. De Lacy is often credited to the actual building of the Carrickfergus Castle although in truth he simply finished the construction begun by De Courcy. It is a sign of the instability of the Norman system, which by now had passed its zenith, that De Lacy himself did not last long. After making Hugh 'Earl of Ulster' in 1205 King John became suspicious of Hugh and his brother Walter. In 1210 King John brought an army to Ulster and, after beseiging Hugh at Carrickfergus Castle, banished him to Scotland.

For a time after the deposition of De Lacy the Earldom of Ulster lay in the King's hands until in time it passed to the De Burgh family. During the 13th century Noman power continued to decline and the links between the settlers in Ireland and the English throne became tenuous indeed with, by the end of the 13th century, the Normans becoming an accepted part of an Irish aristocracy which was becoming more and more restless under English rule.

Robert Bruce, King of Scotland had spent quite some time, between 1306 and 1307, as a refugee on Rathlin Island where it is said he observed the perserverence of a spider which boosted his morale resulting in his victory over Edward II at Bannockburn in 1314. Perhaps as a result of his time on Rathlin, he realised that the Norman influence in Ireland was on the wane and thought it an ideal time to add Ireland to his allies.

He had built up a great relationship with the Irish and in an effort to gain support he wrote to the Irish Kings of Ireland telling them that; *"With God's will you may be able to recover her ancient liberty"*

The Irish Kings were divided in their decision as to whether to accept his 'hand of friendship' but it was pointed out that this was a golden opportunity to throw off the shackles of English dominance. He argued that as the Irish had no real military strength and were dependent on Scottish mercenaries known as 'Gallowglasses' and that as King Robert was also married to the daughter of the Red Earl, Richard de Burgh (Earl of Ulster) at the time, he would be the ideal person to fit the role of liberator. Donal O'Neill led this political movement and his name heads the petition signed by 22 Irish chiefs and sent to Pope John from Dungannon Castle. It denounces the English and laments that as they had no monarch to curb their feudal foe, they had called upon Edward Bruce, brother of Robert Bruce, King of Scotland who was descended from the same ancestors as themselves.

Whether the Irish chiefs' decision to invite him had any influence or not, Robert Bruce's brother, Edward, arrived at Olderfleet (Larne) on 25th May 1315, with 300 ships containing a total of 6,000 veteran soldiers. He was joined by the McDonells and the McSweeney's (whose forefathers had crossed from Galloway and Argyle during the previous century), and marched to Dunedergal (Dunadry) Castle before being joined by other Irish clans – O'Kanes, O'Hanlons, O'Hagans, McGilmores, McCartans and of course the O'Neills. The Castle was destroyed and Rathmore captured. Edward then marched to Dundalk where he was formally crowned 'King of Ireland' on 1st May 1316. During the journey all the Norman settlements on the way were laid waste and disease and famine were prevalent as it is written that:

"they did not leave neither field of corn undestroyed nor towne unsacked nor unfrequented place, were it never soe little nor soe desert, unsearched and unburnt".

The lands around what is now Newtownabbey were destroyed with perhaps the most significant sacrilege being the destruction of the White Abbey.

However not all the Irish families were in favour of Edward and as it became apparent that the hoped for assistance in overthrowing English domination was becoming a bid to rule Ireland, many of the Irish switched allegience away from Edward.

The Normans, who as I have stated had become softened in the ways of war during the long peace which had existed before Bruce's arrival, were thus able to join forces with many of the Irish who had suffered under the new invader to form an opposing force which was led into battle by Richard de Burgh.

The battle took place at Conor, near Ballymena in September but the Anglo-Irish army were no match for the Scottish marauders. They were routed and scattered to various parts of the country. Thomas de Mandeville and his men, pursued by Edward's men, fled to Carrickfergus Castle where, despite attempts to conquer it by siege, they held out for almost a year (September 1315-August 1316).

The town itself was captured by the Scots on Easter Day 1316 when Mandeville made a sally but was killed by one Gilbert Harper. The Anglo-Irish managed to retreat again into the castle to continue their defiance. Inside this castle is a well, which is worth seeing when visiting and, although it supplied fresh water, the food that was necessary for survival was not available, so eventually, the English offered to surrender. Thirty Scots who advanced to take possession of the castle were seized treacherously and made prisoners.

Meanwhile Edward had requested help from his brother Robert, on whose arrival the siege was pressed with more vigour until the internees surrendered in late August, but not before they had endured the horrors of famine, and had even, it is said, eaten the Scottish prisoners.

Edward, full of ambition and lust for additional power, again marched south, through what is now Newtownabbey, towards Dublin and Limerick, laying siege to both towns unsuccessfully. By this time he had lost much support from many of his followers who, quite rightly, recognised him as a merciless invader out to further his own personal ends. A reward of £100 was offered by the Government of Dublin to anyone who:

"Committed any deed against Edward Brice [Bruce], a rebel, being in the land of Ireland, by which he may lost life or limb".

For almost a year he roamed Ireland, travelling between Dundalk and Carrickfergus in particular, before his army was finally defeated and he himself killed at the Battle of Faughart on a hill near Dundalk.

He was beheaded and his head sent to King Edward II on 14th October 1318. The irony of the situation is that his death was greeted with delight by most Irishmen, including the chieftains who had formerly invited his services. An Irishman recorded Bruce's death as:

"There was not done from the beginning of the world a better deed for the men of Irin than that deed; for theft, famine and destruction of men occurred throughout Ireland for the space of three years and a half, and the people used actually to eat one another throughout the island."

After assisting in the defeat of Edward Bruce, Richard de Burgh recovered the lands, which he had previously ruled and when he died in 1326

after an eventful reign of 46 years, he was succeeded to the Ulster Earldom by his grandson William, known as the 'Brown Earl'.

In his attempt to continue his grandfather's efforts to re-establish English law, William made many enemies, amongst them his own distant relatives Robert de Mandeville and John de Logan of Ballywalter (this Ballywalter was near Ballyclare, Co Antrim and was probably named after Walter de Burgh, William's ancestor). This emnity came to a head on the 6th June 1333 when William was assassinated at 'The Earl's Meadow' which was somewhere between Shankill and Carrickfergus. Experts believe it to be about Skegoneill which means 'The Earl's Hawthorne' but a few think it may have occurred at Monkstown, where there was a piece of land until recently actually named 'The Earl's Meadow'.

In Grace's, *'Annals Hiberniae'* it states:

"William de Burgh, Earl of Ulster, was slain by his own relations between the camp at Shankill and Carrickfergus … One Sunday when he was riding to church from the camp of Sancloss (Shankill) to Carrickfergus, the Earl

The People

(Mandeville) *noting that more of his servants were of the Fogan* (Logan) *family than were with the Earl* (of Ulster)*, on the high road while saying morning prayers with him, cleft his skull with a sword stroke from behind."*

With this dastardly crime the story of Norman prosperity in Ireland came to an end, ironically almost on our own doorstep, and forms another important part of Newtownabbey's colourful history.

Although the 15th and 16th centuries saw great upheaval on the mainland with the reign of Henry VIII and the reformation, this part of Ireland remained comparatively quiet until the latter years of the 1500's when, under the reign of Queen Elizabeth, England was taking the first steps on the road to becoming a great Empire. This expansion was driven by a new brand of adventurer such as Raleigh, Drake and Robert Devereaux, the 2nd Earl of Essex who came to Ireland to re-establish English supremacy. He encamped with a large army of approximately 20,000 men at Dunanney on Carnmoney Hill where he is reputed to have held several meetings with Sir Arthur Chichester, finally granting him extensive land in South-East Antrim. Essex was a very close confidant of (some historical scholars say romantically linked with) the Queen but he fell out of favour before completing his task in Ireland and was summoned back to England by Her Majesty where he was tried for treason and executed in 1601 following an attemped 'coup d'etat'.

As part of this process to assert her power in Ireland, Elizabeth had enacted special privileges to encourage settlers, especially from Scotland, to come to Ireland. The Plantation of Ulster was a long, slow, arduous confiscation of land by discreet professional soldiers (like Sir John Chichester, the Governor of Carrickfergus) from Irish peasants. Although the Irish were generally no match for these professionals in battle there were occasional reversals and Chichester was killed in 1597 in an ambush by the MacDonnells at Altfrackyn, near Ballycarry. A little anectdote connected with this assination is told by guides in St. Nicholas' Church when describing the statue over the Tomb. Apparently on a visit to the church by a McDonnell descendant in later years he commented that Chichester should not have a head as his ancestors had removed it – and with that drew his sword and decapitated the statue!

Land and property were given to soldiers as rewards for military action on behalf of Queen Elizabeth. One such property was The White House which was given to Mr Brunker as recorded in a 'noate' in 1574.

By 1601 Sir Arthur Chichester was established as Governor of Carrickfergus Castle (Carrickfergus was still the recognised main town of Ulster with Belfast not receiving its Town Charter until 1613) and within a short period had successfully planted the town with English and Lowland Scots. The town was divided accordingly into English and Scots quarters still recognised today. He also began the building of the town wall in 1608 and the restoration of St. Nicholas' Church (first built in the 12th century) in 1614, but will probably best be remembered by the mansion which he built on the site of the former Franciscan Friary. The only reminder of this house that was called Joymount Palace, is a portion of one of its towers in the courtyard behind the present Town Hall.

To accommodate the increasing Presbyterian population the town's first Presbyterian Church was built in North Street in 1624. However this has to give precedence to the the first Presbyterian Church in 1613 at Ballycarry.

The arrival of the settlers encouraged by Elizabeth, was very much resented by the native Irish and in 1641 this resentment erupted into open rebellion as English and Scots settlers were attacked all over the country. Fearing for their safety, great numbers of settlers from the surrounding areas moved into Carrickfergus until the town was overflowing with refugees. Although many succumbed to starvation and disease due to owercrowding, the town was never actually besieged as Sir Phelim O'Neill and the rebel forces were never able to approach in force.

One of the contributing factors to the timing of the rebellion was the strains which were becoming apparent between the English Parliament and the King. These strains eventually led to the English Civil War and it was the direct repercussions of this which would lead to the shores of Belfast Lough being the scene of events affecting not only Irish but world history as King William III battled with his father-in-law (and uncle), King James II for the throne of England.

The People

The Williamite Wars in Ireland really began in 1689 with the arrival of Frederick, Duke of Schomberg, (a very experienced soldier who had fought on many European battlefields) at Groomsport, Co. Down. His army besieged Carrickfergus Castle for a week beginning 20th August of that year and gained possession when Colonel Charles McKarty Moore surrendered. However, Schomberg's campaign was greatly curtailed by deaths in the ranks of his army through dreaded pestilence and lack of equipment and he was therefore in no position to face the threat of James II's army which was marching northward for a confrontation.

It was therefore inevitable that King William III, himself a very notable successful military soldier and tactician, would come to Ireland in an attempt to thwart King James II. Schomberg and his army, albeit depleted, awaited the arrival of His Majesty by encamping on Carnmoney Hill and on what is now Station Road, Whiteabbey (on the site now occupied by Fernagh), overlooking the lough and awaiting the Kings' arrival. At that time there was no O'Neill Road or Doagh Road; the latter not being constructed until 1812. King William III arrived on 14th June 1690 and Gideon Bonaverte (after whom a local park is named), Scribe to His Majesty, records it in his diary on 16th June, 1690.

"The general (Schomberg) *expecting the King's landing, came here on Friday afternoon and sent men to all adjacent coasts to watch and at nine o'clock the post boy from Donaghadee brought advice that the King had passed.*

On Saturday about three o'clock in the afternoon the general received advice that the King was come into the Lough and thereupon in his coach and set of small Barbary horses, posted away to meet the King at Carrickfergus.

The King immediately after landing mounted his horse and rode through the streets of the town, where almost numberless crowds received him with continued shouts and acclamations until The White House where he met the General's carriage at four o'clock. He was pleased then to dismount and to enter the coach which, attended by one troop of horse rode over the strand to Belfast. As the King was driving over the strand another coach met him, which His Grace called to and ordered to be driven straight forward to White

House to receive such persons of quality as they should find landing.

The lough between this and Carrickfergus seems like a wood, there being no less than 700 ships of sail in it, mostly laden with provisions and ammunition. The plenty and order of all things here is most wonderful and scarcely credible to those who witness it."

I have had the honour of personally handling and examining this diary in the British Museum and found it most enlightening.

Today, over 300 years later the repercussions of the Williamite Wars including the Battle of the Boyne still haunts the people of Ireland. One section of the community argues that it was the end of catholic equality while another section celebrates a 'victory' which was supposed to guarantee freedom of religion and liberty for all William's subjects.

Whatever the outcome of the Williamite wars, a mere hundred years later, at the end of the 18th century, the entire western world was ready for radical social change. Changes in political thinking where the common people demanded equality and justice resulted in the French Revolution and the American War of Independence.

This revolutionary fervour found fertile ground in Ireland where the penal laws were resented by Presbyterian and Catholic alike.

These Penal Laws forbid Catholics to serve Mass or hold any offices of importance, like medicine, teaching, military or banking. Presbyterians were not much better off with their clergy not officially recognised and therefore any of their burial, marriage or christening services were deemed to be illegal. The main means of earning a living was farming and because they were paying exorbitant rents to 'absentee landlords', many of whom had never even set foot in Ireland, many people emigrated to begin a new life in America, which was fast becoming recognised as the land of opportunity. The emigrants usually sailed from Belfast, Larne or Londonderry on a six-week journey in ships that got the name of 'coffin ships' because of the atrocious conditions. They were so crowded that fevers claimed many lives during a crossing and sometimes the hatches were closed throughout the journey to avoid the spread of disease.

These emigrants played a major part in the formation of the United States where they gained an outstanding reputation as fearless soldiers. They were also to the forefront in their willingness to dig ditches, make roads and railways and in general do everything within their power to develop their new-found homeland. It is from this Ulster Scot stock that U.S.A. has got at least twelve Presidents, amongst them Andrew Jackson. Undoubtedly their letters home inspired those they had left to fight for better conditions.

A young Protestant barrister from Dublin, Theobald Wolfe Tone, argued that Ireland should have a national government and to this end got involved in establishing the Society of United Irishmen. Initially the United Irishmen were prepared to attain their goal by peaceful persuasion but the political reforms did not come quick enough and the radicals began to organise themselves into an army containing both catholics and protestants. Its leaders included Jemmy (James) Hope from Roughfort and Henry Joy McCracken a young man who was thrown in as an emergency Northern Leader after the resignation of Robert Simms.

Several key battles in the 1798 uprising were fought in Southeast Antrim, events I explore more fully in the sections on The Roughfort and The Liberty Tree which summarise the unsuccessful uprising. To judge the events of 1798 it is suffice to quote Charles Dickson in *'Revolt in North Antrim and Down',*

"Let it not be forgotten that successful insurrection is known to the world as 'revolution' and the new rulers enjoy the advantage of writing the official history of their time. Unsuccessful insurrection, on the other hand, is a 'criminal conspiracy' and the aims and characters of the defeated participants are duly nullified: Washington is extolled and Wolfe Tone is execrated"!

Compared to the upheavals of the previous centuries, for the north shore of the lough the 19th and 20th centuries passed relatively quietly. The effects of The Act of the Union in 1801, the Famine in the mid 1840's and many other important dates were over shadowed in this area by the effects of the inexorable growth of Belfast.

From the granting of Carrickfergus' charter by King John in 1210 (renewed by Elizabeth in 1569) Belfast had always remained in the shadow of the sea-side town. However by the mid 1800s and the coming of the industrial revolution, Belfast began to gain prominence through its industries, finally gaining City status in 1888. By the beginning of the 20th century it had the biggest shipbuilding, the biggest tobacco factory, the biggest linen industry and the biggest ropeworks in the world – quite an achievement for such a small city! It was perhaps coincidental or perhaps a reflection on its aspirations that in the year of its centenary celebrations, Belfast had its youngest Sovereign, Mayor or Lord Mayor in its history in the 29 year old, Nigel Dodds.

The citizens residing along the north shore could only look on as in 1912 one of the products of this industry, the White Star liner 'Titanic' sailed from its birthplace at Belfast shipyard, Harland & Wolff, down Belfast Lough to the tumultuous cheers and jollifications of thousands of well-wishers who had congregated on the Lough shore. They waved makeshift flags and banners. The ship actually stayed just off the coast at Carrickfergus overnight before continuing on its fateful journey never to return to its homeland.

On 'Ulster Day' 28th September 1912 over 218,000 people signed the Covenant at Belfast City Hall against Home Rule. They were determined to object to self government as continously lobbied for by people from southern Ireland as against the wishes of the majority of northerners. However, even this important political issue was put on hold by the outbreak of The Great War. Many thousands of young men (or should I say boys) who had been active in the Ulster Volunteer Fighters movement founded to oppose 'Home Rule' decided to use the opportunity to put their acquired skills to use by taking the King's shilling. What they believed would be the 'adventure of a lifetime' in reality cost many of them their lives.

On the 1st July 1916 at the Battle of the Somme the local 36th Ulster Division fort along side so many thousands of others regardless of politics or religion with unbelievable and unforgettable consequences. Thousands perished and as a token of respect it was suggested by Sir Crawford McCullagh (who lived at Lismara, Whiteabbey and

The People

who served 18 years as Lord Mayor of Belfast) that Belfast City Council should acknowledge the catastrophe by two minutes silence in remembrance of the fallen heroes thus instigating the 'two minute silence' now practised throughout the world on other occasions.

Many other distinguished people have resided within this area's boundaries. Charles Lanyon, one of the world's leading architects lived at 'The Abbey' and James Mackie the textile machinery manufacturer had his family home at Hazelbank. Thomas Gallaher rose from a young boy of twelve years of age in charge of over 50 employees in a cigar manufacturing company in Londonderry to become the entrepreneur and owner of the world's largest tobacco company. He lived at Ballygoland House on the Whitewell Road and is remembered affectionately by the locals as Old Tom.

His next-door neighbour on the Whitewell Road was one of Ireland's greatest poets Sir Samuel Ferguson. Other famous people from the area who spring to mind are Stephen Boyd, originally William Millar the famous international actor and film star who was born on 4th July 1931 at Doagh Road corner, Whitehouse, and not Glengormley as many people believe. Paddy Hopkirk the world champion rally driver who put the Mini Cooper on the 'map' learnt his skills as a schoolboy when his brother pushed him past William Millars house on Doagh Road on a makeshift 'guider', a type of cart.

The author Archibald McIlroy who was drowned on the ill-fated Lusitania, Florence Mary McDowell a brilliant author of childhood reminiscences and stories used in the school's curriculum, who did not write her first book *'Other Days Around Me'* until she was 83 years of age. Joseph Gillis Biggar from Mallusk, the controversial M.P. for Cavan (1874) is remembered for his argumentative personality typified in The Times of 17th January 1867 which carries an interesting anecdote:–

Biggar (the Irish politician) used to remove his boots at all-night sittings. Disraeli was seated on the bench in front of Biggar, who placed one of his stockinged feet on the back of the bench on each side of Disraeli's head, with the most comical effect. "What is happening?" enquired one of Disraeli's friends who had just entered the House. "We fear for foot and mouth disease" responded Disraeli in sepulchral tones.

Biggar was very involved in the Fenian movement and in an effort to stop the adaption of legislation detrimental to his cause he once made a speech in Parliament of what is believed to have been 11 hours and would not 'give way' to other members. He was also sued for Breach of Promise and was fined £400 and his life is summed up by saying that he was an unmarried Presbyterian-Fenian, turned Catholic, buried from St. Patricks Catholic Church in Donegall Street, Belfast, to a Church of Ireland Cemetery by a Roman Catholic Priest.

Another controversial local was Lilian Bland the grand-daughter of the Dean of Belfast who designed, built and flew her own aeroplane in 1910 - 1911, making her the first Irish woman to fly, and probably the first in the world to build an aeroplane. During her building she called it Mayfly saying that *"It may fly and it may not"*, and used her aunt's ear trumpet to feed the fuel to the engine. She was a type of tomboy wearing breeches instead of dresses and rode astride her horse as against the usual side-saddle preferred by other ladies. Yet, if this summary gives the impression that she was anything other than beautiful one has only to see her photograph to appreciate her good looks.

At the end of the World War II after all the uncertainty it was the beginning of a new dawn with the worries of war forgotten, it was the intention of the Government to try and provide better housing facilities for everyone. It was their intention to do away with the old Edwardian terraced houses and provide better housing and commerical properties. Belfasts' expansion of the late 19th century had continued unabated, its population exploded, spreading its tentacles outwards in all directions. It is surely ironic that the overspill from the Belfast (for so many centuries the junior town along the north shore of the lough) would result in changes to the landscape which would dwarf any that had gone before.

To accommodate the housing needs of the capital city, by the late 40s several housing developments were under way with the major one, Rathcoole, being one of the largest in Europe at the time. By the mid 50's the population of the area was becoming too large to be comfortably administered by Belfast Rural District Council and it suggested the formation of a 'new town' north of the city. As a result of this on the 1st April 1958 Newtownabbey was designated as the first town in Ireland to be formed by a British Act of Parliament.

The People

The original seven villages that formed Newtownabbey Urban District Council in 1958 were Whitehouse, Whiteabbey, Whitewell, Jordanstown, Monkstown, Glengormley and Carnmoney.

On the reorganisation of local government in 1973, Newtownabbey was amongst many other areas which were dramatically changed, its status being altered from Newtownabbey Urban District Council to Newtownabbey District Council and its boundaries extensively enlarged to include Ballyclare (previously under the auspices of Antrim District Council), Ballynure and Straid, therefore making Newtownabbey at 54 sq miles, one of the biggest and most densely populated in Northern Ireland. In 1977 it was granted Borough status with a Mayor and has proved to be one of the most progressive in Northern Ireland.

While the focus of activity in the 20th century seems to have been on Belfast and Newtownabbey, Carrickfergus was by no means idle with its ambitions. At the same time as retaining its historical prominence it developed quite a considerable industrial reputation with the opening of the ICI man-made fibres manufacturing plant at Kilroot, Rothmans cigarette factory at Seapark and Courtaulds which mirrored the hopes of mass employment of the Michelin factory at Mallusk. Unfortunately the vagaries of the marketplace meant that the star of these great multinational-owned factories, though bright, was short-lived and the last two decades have seen a serious decline in the industrial base. However, if we have learned anything in our brief trip through the turbulent history of this little part of Ireland it is that nothing stays the same. Already the seeds of regeneration in the form of numerous, locally-owned small businesses are starting to flower, both in the abandoned premises of these former giants and in the many industrial parks the area now boasts. I have no doubt that, drawing on the same qualities of entrepeneurial tenacity displayed by their fore fathers the people of this area can look forward to a bright and prosperous future.

On reflection this strip of land along the shore where man first set foot in Ireland, has played a prominent part in moulding Irish history. We hope that the parts we have chosen to feature are representative of its proud history.

They are all there to be appreciated and admired. I hope you enjoy your journey through time.

Dear Reader

This book is from our much complimented illustrated book series which includes:-

Belfast	Dundalk & North Louth
By the Lough's North Shore	Drogheda & the Boyne Valley
East Belfast	Blanchardstown, Castleknock and the Park
South Belfast	Dundrum, Stillorgan & Rathfarnham
Antrim, Town & Country	Limerick's Glory
Inishowen	Galway on the Bay
Donegal Highlands	Armagh
Donegal, South of the Gap	Ring of Gullion
Fermanagh	The Mournes
Omagh	Heart of Down
Cookstown	Strangford Shores

**Cottage Publications
is an imprint of
Laurel Cottage Ltd
15 Ballyhay Road
Donaghadee, Co. Down
N. Ireland, BT21 0NG**

For the more athletically minded our illustrated walking book series includes:-

Bernard Davey's Mourne	Tony McAuley's Glens
Bernard Davey's Mourne Part 2	

Also available in our 'Illustrated History & Companion' Range are:-

City of Derry	Holywood	Ballymoney
Lisburn	Banbridge	

And from our Music series:-

Colum Sands, Between the Earth and the Sky

We can also supply prints, individually signed by the artist, of the paintings featured in the above titles as well as many other areas of Ireland.

For details on these superb publications and to view samples of the paintings they contain, you can visit our web site at **www.cottage-publications.com** or alternatively you can contact us as follows:-

Telephone: +44 (028) 9188 8033   Fax: +44 (028) 9188 8063